A Decent Truth

First Edition Design Publishing

A Decent Truth
Copyright ©2013 James Evans
ISBN 978-1622873-75-3 PRINT
ISBN 978-1622-873-74-6 EBOOK

LCCN 2013946353

July 2013

Published and Distributed by
First Edition Design Publishing, Inc.
P.O. Box 20217, Sarasota, FL 34276-3217
www.firsteditiondesignpublishing.com

Cover Design by Deborah E Gordon

Acknowledgements

Before I thank everyone, I must thank the Most High first, for giving me the knowledge, understanding and wisdom I needed to put this work together. I thank my mother Betty C Evans, My father Carl Evans, Sr. I also want to thank my step father Jason Cotterll, all the brothers and sisters of my parents and those who believe strongly in what I put together. I want to thank those who said that I would never be anything in life. I thank my ex-wife Varonica Totress and her family, all thirteen of my children, as well as their mothers and mothers' mothers and fathers. I thank those who support my book and grow from it. I thank you as well. Keep growing and building. Last but not least I would like to thank my publisher, Deborah Gordon, for giving me the chance to be a part of First Edition Design Publishing, and Curtis E. Page for taking the time to edit my book.

P.S. I also thank all those that came before me and those who are sure to come after.

Dedications

This book is first and foremost dedicated to God. I also dedicate it to the one person who has always loved me and been at my side through all my pitfalls in life, my mother Betty Evans Cottrell. To my father Carl James Evans, Sr. My grandparents Viola Evans, Jesse Evans, Varamay Wallace and Clarence Wallace, Sr. To my aunt/mom Oritha Johnson who still lives in my hometown Omaha, Nebraska, to all of my children and their mothers. Last but not least, To La La and Channelle, my brothers and sisters, Felicia Vaughn, Angela Benson, Abraham L. Salter, Carl James Evans, Jr., Dawn Evans, Ronald Johnson R.I.P. and also my baby brothers Clarence and Clayton Evans.

Why I Wrote the Book

I wrote this book, because I found it necessary to help awaken the walking dead. Although this book is written to help the black unconscious mind become conscious, it applies to every one of every race. Even though things were said before my time, I found it necessary to remind those that had forgotten and fallen back asleep. I also wrote this, because I, myself, have children. This was put together for the welfare of all children, but also to help remind myself of where I've been and where I'm going.

People today are so lost, that they're willing to accept anything, no matter how outrageous it may sound. So being that I was blessed with sound mind and knowledge while incarcerated, it became a must that I do my part for my dark nation. When a people have no self-knowledge, nor knowledge of their heritage, pride becomes non-existent. In order for one to grow, they must have the right tools to help them go the direction they want to, as well as should, be going. We must stop blaming others for our downfalls, why we are here or there, because ultimately we are destroying ourselves. It is my hope that those who read this will come to a clear understanding of who they are, where they come from and where they are going, to take what they have learned and share it with the next person.

Table of Contents

The Drug Addict

Addicted to death and no way home
Your conscience slipping away
  Like the day skies falling into the abyss of night
Consequences of your actions have cast you away
  From the loving arms of a family who surely mourns the lost
A child looks into his mother's beautiful eyes
  Knowing that his mother's in there somewhere
His contempt isn't for her
  It's for what she has become
Not knowing the conspiracy is
  Working on him too
The pushing of contraband into
  Our neighborhoods is the working
Of the unseen hand

So Addicted to the consumption of death
  She is unwilling to do right by her young ones
But in truth her cries for help
  Are unseen and unheard
Her dreams gone
  With the first pull and stick in the arm
Thinking she has found the answer
  To her emotional pains
But quickly reality sets in
  Like a swift kick in the ass
Scarred and too ashamed to go home
  And see the child of the family
For she knows she'll be rejected
  In some shape
  Or an unwelcoming mutated form

Of chastisement
So she allows her conscience
  To slide back into darkness
Forever lost in a world that doesn't exist
  Yet it's real to her
Not knowing of all the love
  She has left behind
Allowing the false pride within
  To mislead her down a path
Of caring for nothing and no one
  Not even herself
The self-destruction
  Of such a precious soul
Is so unsettling to watch
  The child closes his eyes
  To remember the good times
Contrary to what she believes
  He still loves her
Even though she's
  The Drug Addict

Necromongers

The unsettling reality is that we are all drug addicts. This is a truth we must all face. It doesn't matter what the 'drug' is (alcohol, beer, pills, cannabis, black or anything). We all delude our minds and mental state with some form of mutagenic drug. No matter what the reason for using (stress, depression, etc.), it gives you a passing grade. If you don't have it at least once a day, you feel that your day isn't going right.

This is the lie we tell ourselves to justify our actions. In many cases we end up making our lives worse than they should be. The unseen powers prefer it this way, because our focus isn't on them and their actions.

We have fallen into a pattern of self-destruction generation after generation. This is all due to the trick knowledge of Willy Lynch. He showed the slave owners how to keep the slaves in check, to do it by breaking their spirit and keeping their Negro souls bound in chains. These chains were not physical.

Willy Lynch was a British slave owner. He was invited to the colony of Virginia in 1712. William Lynch claimed to know how to control a slave without brutality. His methods were proven to work in 1712 and still work to this day. He outlined to the American slave owners how it worked. He showed how to turn the young black slave against the old black slave, the male black slave against the female black slave, the dark skin slave against the light skin slave. He showed how to make the slave trust the master (white man) more than their own kind. Willy Lynch is responsible for the making of the so-called Negro. He made the Negro by breaking their pride, stripping them of self-respect, crushing their morale, their heritage, etc.

In his letter, Willy Lynch pointed out that by following his methods, the American slave owner would never again have to force the slave to do anything. The Negro will destroy himself/herself. If the methods were used correctly it would work for hundreds of years to come (which it has to this day). He likened it to breaking a horse, by his words. "Both the Nigger and the horse must be broken," Willy Lynch said. It was breaking them of one form of mentality to instill another form into them. "Keep the boy. Take the mind." In other words, break the will to exist. If you break the female, she, in turn, will break the child.

Many of the actions to break the slaves were violent and inhuman. Black people are more likely to turn on themselves than on their oppressors, because of Willy Lynch. They will protect those that are white over those that are black. We are more likely to kill ourselves mentally, spiritually and physically before anyone else, yet turn around and blame White America. The cold part about this, is that some blacks will say they know, but they just don't give a damn. Most of us are still doing this subconsciously. What was done, can be undone, but we as a people must do this ourselves. We must "let go and let God."

In 1984, the KKK congratulated blacks for killing more of our own than whites did in slavery times. In the present, we still haven't done much better. Willy Lynch must die. His ideas and methods formulated in his letter "The Making of a Slave" must be forgotten.

There is a reason why there are six liquor stores on every corner within four blocks in the ghettos, slums and projects. The word I choose to use, Necromonger, comes from "The Chronicles of Riddick". In the movie the word is used to describe a race of people. The meaning of the word is, "That which will convert or kill". Split the word in two. You then have Necro and monger. Go to the dictionary and you will find these definitions.

Necro: 1. Death. 2. The dead.
Monger: 1. A dealer

These death dealers not only make deals with the dead, they practice necromancy, which is the art that claims to communicate with the spirits/souls of the dead to predict the future. The man who leads these death dealers is called "the Holy Half Dead".

Now look at the word democracy or democrat. The first word is *demo* or *de*

> **De**: reverse action, get rid of
> **Demo**: People
> **Cracy**: Government; rule.
> *This word comes from the Greek word Kratos, meaning power or god of war.*

> **Crat**: A participant in or supporter of a specified form of government.
> *This word comes from the French word Crate, meaning member of a dominant class.*

Now take a moment and stop and think about this. We have the people who work in and for the American Government, called democrats, who are the participants and supporters of this ruling body. The ruling body is made up of the Necromongers. They don't outright say, "If we can't convert you, we will kill you," they say, "We come in peace." They always say the latter.

Are they all bad? No. Then are they all good? Hell no! They are the ones who allow drugs, guns and alcohol into our neighborhoods. They take out any positive influence in the ghettos in order to keep the Negros from rising into greatness once again. The Negro is anyone and everyone who won't convert.

Our government is run by death dealers, and we the common people, are the so called Negros. The word Negro comes from Necro which comes from Necrot. A Necrot is a mentally and spiritually dead person. The common people's souls are bound in chains and being devoured by Americana, the serpent deity. The bible speaks of this in Revelations. The Necromongers justify this by seeing it as the ends justifying the means. As long as they dance the dance of Necromancy, they feel their future is guaranteed. They feed the serpent the souls of the walking Necrot/Negro.

To take all the tools of death out of the ghettos would be to go against all they stand for. The Necromongers are a demonic people. Believe it or not, they have divine demonic powers given to them by Americana.

While we are poisoning ourselves with these mutagenic drugs, they are busy setting up for the New World Order. Anything can become a drug to people, even money. The drug that I speak of is anything that causes one's own mental state to become altered from its normal functions; and the drug will transform your mentality as well as your own souls. You will become destructive to everyone around you as well as to yourself.

How many people in the ghettos, slums and projects do you know that can afford a treatment center or some form of counseling. You know none, because we can't afford it at any level. The powers know this and thrive upon it. We only get worse until there is no fight left in our spirit. Then the soul is no more, not even a memory. Drugs of any kind will take S.E.L.F. from being a Supreme Eternal Life Form to an Eternal Life Form to a mire form. After that it's anyone's best guess. You don't want to reach that point, because it would mean that you have mutated into something so unrecognizable that no one would recognize you, save for family and friends. Yet even with them, they would recognize only a small part of you, having watched you transform through your ugly mutation; and their best guess is that you're in there somewhere.

These Necromongers are bent on world population control by any means necessary, as my mother Betty C. Evans would say, "By hook or by crook." As the Borg would say on Star Trek,

"Resistance is futile." The Borg is very similar to the real-life Necromongers. If they can't bring you into the collective, they'll kill you emotionlessly without a second thought. Remember, the ends justify the means, right? In other words, you don't matter, and they don't mind. There is genius in their madness, one must admit. Therefore it will take an even greater genius to stop these death dealers. It will take a thief in the night to give us back what we lost, which is our pride, self-worth, heritage, knowledge, souls and being/existence.

Notes:

A Thief in the Night

Emerging from the shadows of this world
    Snatching the demonic souls
    Casting them into the lowest part of purgatory
Like a thief in the night
    Robbing his victim within the blink of an eye
I follow not the whispers in the wind
    Come from the serpent
    My mantra is strong
It creeps upon us like a hungry lion
    Stalking its prey
By the prickling in my thumb I feel
    This way something wicked comes

The comprehension of life's matrix
    Confusing to the intellect of mankind
However, there is a Higher Power
    That guides us all
We were created from the dust of the earth
    Molded into shape from sounding clay
My mother is Earth
Every time you throw my body to the ground
    It only makes me stronger
Murder I cry
    With blood in my eye

I'm coming for you Necromongers
    To snatch your evil souls
    To cast them into the lowest part of purgatory.

Before they robbed us of our souls, they first gave up their own. It takes a soulless person to plan population control, biological and chemical warfare, upon a people who are only guilty for being fools for believing the government has our best interest at heart. That is not their interest.

The first action to take is to educate your S.E.L.F. and those around you to find a solution as to how to stop this mental warfare (or should I say psychological warfare) before any more damage is done to us and our black youth. Take it from one who's locked away. I know full well that prison is what happens to a dream deferred, that the graveyard is what happens to a dream gone away.

The mental enslavement of the masses must not go unchecked. You can best believe the resurrection of the mentally walking dead will not be on any news, shows or radio stations. I sit at times and walk around watching the deaf, dumb and blind aimlessly wandering around, not knowing what's to come. At times it's very unsettling to watch, as well as a bit heart breaking, because you know that no matter what you say, they'll stay the way they are. In some cases they'll hate you for even telling them.

> "Speak not in the ears of a fool,
> For he will despise the wisdom
> Of your words."
> -Solomon-

This is the folly of the myth and saying, "ignorance is bliss" and "blind faith will get us to heaven". To point out a small, but simple truth is very hurtful, because we've become so comfortable with the lies told to us since childhood. A Necrot is willing to fight and die to uphold that foolishness forced upon us by the serpent and his (demo)crats.

The Walking Necrot

The walking dead are those
      So called Negros who are unaware
      Of their own existence
Zombies, more harmful to the eternal self
      Destructive to all they touch
Their consciousness stagnated
      As a dream deferred
The plague of Willy Lynch
      Still wreaking havoc upon the black soul
 As some souls awaken, they feel as though
      They have taken a quantum leap
      Through time and space
As if they have shifted
      Through alternate realities
The walking dead
      Is a constant reminder
Of a recurring nightmare
      That one's own consciousness
      Can't escape from
The resurrection of the walking Necrot
      Has begun
The symbolic living dead
      Eating the flesh of their own people
It's what the black child
      Is doing to his or her own people
Preying upon each other like cannibals
      Doing unspeakable things
      To survive another day
The re-genesis of the once walking dead

Is what the unseen powers are trying to prevent
By altering our genetic make-up
With the many poisons in our neighborhoods
So to look deformed to the naked eyes
Let the resurrection of the walking dead begin
Let the resurrection begin
The genius of a great people
Is most feared by Jinn
Our re-genesis back into the world
They will not allow
It is said to let the dead bury the dead
How many must we bury before we awaken?
Let the resurrection of the walking Necrot begin…

Family

"One has to face their
Own fears or forever run
From them."
-Hyemeyo Storm

"Ones family is like a
Nation. For a nation
To run with very few
Mistakes, all must work
Together as a unit.
The myth of tough love
Has never worked
For any of us.
Family means 'together'..."
-James Evans Sr.

Notes:

Moving On

Moving on into a world
       Without the ones who swore to love me
I walked through the door
       Only to find I've been left behind
All because of the strange cravings
       Of my flesh
I dropped into the abyss of loneliness
       Heart aches, stress and despair
As I lay at night the tears run down my face
       Like rushing water flowing down a mountain stream
Forced into a life on the streets
       That wasn't of my choosing
Hated for not loving
       According to the social norm
I am still precious
       And a child loved by the Most High
Although you've left me behind
       I still love you all and wish you well
No longer allowing my mental to linger on
       In the negative state it was left
So I'll be moving on.

The structure of the strong black family has been violently and savagely ripped out by its roots and replaced with an abundance of plagues, to ensure that the emergence of (or should I say, "To ensure that the re-emergence of") strength, togetherness, pride and knowledge of self stays blank within black families and youth, to make it almost impossible for our homes to be rebuilt on firm ground.

What is tough love really? Who has it actually helped? Growing up there was no such thing as tough love. There was only love and loving harder when a family member was fallen by the wayside. It didn't matter if your child or family member was gay, on drugs, an alcoholic, etc. We loved them, even if it was at a distance. They could always take shelter and come back home for a time.

Now we've learned this new thing called "Tough Love", which means you must cast your loved one away and abandon them at every level. Love no longer exists within our hearts. We are quick to say, "I'm a God-fearing person," but didn't God say, "Think not that you can say you believe in Me, love Me and fear Me and think you would not be tested." God also says, "If you truly love Me, then you will love My creation." We have been manipulated into taking on this act of showing tough love to our dear ones, thinking good will come of it. Yet the very people who fool us into this nonsense do just the opposite.

Your family is your nation, tribe and unit. It takes all of us working together to make our society run smoothly. We are each other's father, mother, brother, sister, aunt, uncle, nephew, niece, cousin, etc. We must re-educate ourselves and each other, now and for the future generations that are on their way. For each of us that miss educating the next one, we are to blame for the misfortune of our youth, who rely on information to guide them past the bullshit in society and the trick knowledge of Willy Lynch. Our youth must be shown how to slip past and avoid this mental and spiritual death.

Without each other we have nothing. Far too many of us are willing to abandon a loved one based on sexuality, drugs, alcohol or betrayal of the heart or whatever. Yes, we have been hurt, but that's when you get real and stand your ground for your family, letting them know this, "Bring it on, because I won't give up on you or let you go." Let them know you are more than willing to go down swinging for them in our dark nation. Tough love should mean, "Love them more," not, "Love them less and abandon them."

Right now we are not balanced in our home for this reason: we are not balanced in our own souls. This unbalance comes from an abundance of misinformation and lack of knowledge about the existing S.E.L.F. Women, especially black women, have fallen for that I-don't-need-a-black-man syndrome. Black men are on this break-a-bitch bullshit. It's this backward ass thinking that has our families in such disarray.

In today's times, secrets within families will ultimately destroy us all. It's very true that "three may keep a secret if two are dead." With the deep issues in our homes, we don't need secrets. What we need is truth. The only secrets we should keep are those from our enemies/frienemies. They don't need to know, lest they harm us.

When a loved one gets lost in the wilderness, you or I must become that symbolic North Star and guide them back to safety, back into the family fold. We can't allow these Necromongers to dictate to us on how our families should be formed. Resistance is not futile. It is that very resistance within us that can change the world we live in.

Another word for resistance is revolution. Without it the very conditions of our living will never change, will never get better. We must understand one thing: there is no one way to fight a war, battle or revolution. No one method is the only way. There will always be resistance in our families to change the thinking, but what good is a revolution when you know not what you're fighting for. One can't argue mixed fruit in the middle of war.

The seven laws of Kwanzaa (Imani: Faith, Umoja: Unity, Kujichagulia: Self-Determination, Ujamaa: Cooperative

Economics, Nia: Purpose, Kuumba: Creativity) are the keys to holding our families together. Children are another key to our strength and future, but if poorly educated they become as dust in the wind, a hindrance and helpful to no one, not even themselves. Backwards thinking must not be our self-annihilation. At this point we are on that road. However, with the re-genesis of the consciousness within the black mind will emerge once again as the most blessed creation to ever exist.

We must use the keys given to us. One more key is our women. As the saying goes, behind every great man, there's a great woman. Barack Obama has three great women. A son wouldn't be a bad addition either. Nonetheless, the New World Order is what it is.

The knowledge of self is a key we must acquire before we can get a feel as to the direction we need to go in. Self-knowledge is the only way to truly know your Creator. The Necromongers made a race of Negro who followed the trick knowledge of Willy Lynch. They have developed a resistance against wanting to know and resented those who choose to accept the light. They have grown accustomed to not resisting our oppressors and to waging war upon each other for the unseen powers who promise riches for those who convert. A family divided cannot stand and will surely come to a most unwilling, unwelcomed end.

Having a family is much like a relationship, because without key points it cannot and will not grow. An issue within our families is that we don't communicate with each other. The key to any relationship is a level of communication. No relationship can ever survive without open conversation on every level. This is the reason there is no trust within families: there are way too many secrets. Parents keep to the old saying that children must be seen but never heard. They brow beat them, but never listen. When that happens, you get gang members, drug addicts, alcoholics, teenage parents, etc. living in our homes. There is absolutely no balance in our nation.

Look at the black families today and you will see that within each small nation, tribe and unit we are, and have been, eroding away for far too long. It is time we bring about a rebirth of black family values. We must bring order out of chaos.

You have a gay, lesbian, bi-sexual, transgender and a heterosexual. Which one of us is better? Of course the heterosexual would say he is and that the other sexualities are not his family, because what they do is a sin against God. I would say to him, "You have sinned against God as well, brother."

H.S. "They have sex, men with men and women with women."

P.J. "OK, but you are an adulterer."

H.S. "You can't go to heaven doing that."

P.J. "You can't get there passing judgment."

H.S. "You're sick."

P.J. "You're a liar."

H.S. "God said you shouldn't do that."

P.J. "God also said love your neighbor."

H.S. "You all have broken the commandment."

P.J. "And you have broken several commandments."

H.S. "How can you love them?"

P.J. "God said I am my brother's and sister's keeper and I should forgive 70 times 70."

H.S. "Repent sinner!"

P.J. "I do, but there's something in your eye."

H.S. "Accept Christ or go to Hell."

P.J. "I accept none but God and respect all the prophets."

H.S. "You're going to Hell."

P.J. "OK. If I go first, I'll hold a seat for you."

H.S. "I'm a child of God. I'm going to Heaven."

P.J. "Yes. We are all children of God, but don't be so sure you're getting through those gates."

My point in doing this back and forth is to show that no matter what fault you may find in one person, there are four more upon yourself. No one is better than the other, except by one way and one way only. Depending on how we use it makes the difference between us becoming angels or demons. We are only superior to each other in a consciousness of degrees.

We can't decide who should or should not be a part of the resistance based on small differences, when we are all fighting for the same thing. In the time of real revolution it takes a mixture of all kinds to win. So arguing about mixed fruit gets us nowhere. We should not be so fast to exclude a family member based on a difference in his/her lifestyle or thinking, be he/she rich or poor, educated or uneducated. No one should be left behind. We ALL must remain strong in the face of adversity.

Stand Strong Soldier

Dark clouds hang above
       Confusion rests upon our shoulders
The question whispers
       From the winds of our mouths
Who am I and where do I go from here?

To know is to have the truths
       To what is
Having no doubts to one's own existence
A soldier must stand strong
       In the face of Necromongers

       Stand strong soldier
For the time to rest is not now
       Who shall carry on with our truth
If you should slumber now

       Stand strong soldier
Knowing that when you're alone
       You are not alone
Your strength is my strength
       And my strength is your strength
To own

       The twisted realities of society
May blind the path
       In which one wishes to walk
But there is a candle inside the window
       Lighting the way
The light

The light
Where is the light which is to guide us all
Let go of your rage
        Let your wrath be upon the unrighteous

A soldier must stand strong
        In the face of Necromongers

Stand strong soldier
        Stand strong

Our battle here has come to its end
        But our war is yet to begin
So you must stand strong soldier
        You must stand strong.

A rather simple truth is no matter what we may think, or what we are told we are all connected to each other. So to call a black man a soul brotha and a black woman a soul sista has a greater meaning to it than one realizes. In a sense we do know we're family, but we have no idea of the truth of such statements, soul brotha and soul sista. I believe that if we truly understood our deep connection, we would be more respectful and loving towards one another.

One thing you must also know is that your own family member can be a frienemy. The worst frienemy of all is your own self. You are your own worst enemy. The sad truth is that most of the time we never realize it. Those few that know do care. Your family can't grow if one link is unbalanced or disconnected from the whole collective. In that scenario, very few of us keep moving in the right direction.

Family doesn't always mean the people we were born into blood with. Sometimes it's the friends we make in life, which in many cases, turn out for better. In some cases our outside choice of friends can be the wrong one. We could be letting a lion into our families. Wherever things appear to be heading, they might not end up at the expected point. Family means together, one unit, one nation, all for one and one for all.

"YES WE CAN!!"

Notes:

There Were More than One

"The civil rights movement was won
By Martin Luther King Jr.
With non-violence…
If you don't knock it off!"
-James Evans Sr.

For the first time a slave decided to run for his freedom here in this strong land, it was the birth of resistance to the harsh, savage conditions of a lost people. Slaves ran, because they had a dream; a dream of being freed from these bringers of death. Their dream caused a chain reaction in the lost nation of Muslims who came from so-called Africa. Slaves wanted the God-given human rights they were born with and were willing to die for it.

The resistance/revolution didn't start with, nor did it end with, Martin Luther King, Jr. Yet the Necromongers want us to believe it did, so we can be non-violent. That's something I don't agree with, but there is more than one way to fight a revolution. Being non-violent toward my violent oppressors, who commit savage acts against me, causing me to commit savage acts toward *my own people*, doesn't sit right with me. There is something very wrong with that.

Malcolm X, born Malcolm Little in Omaha, Nebraska on May 19th, 1925, became a member of the nation of Islam once released from prison in 1956. God blessed him with the gift of pure knowledge and wisdom, thus making him the favorite of Elijah (Robert Pool) Muhammad. Elijah helped him build a new nation of people in the 60's. Blacks became more than the small, unworthy people they felt themselves to be, to knowing they are the black Asiatic race; from the Negro, to the so-called Negro; from the lost, to the lost, found nation; from nothing, to somebody; from third-eye blind, to raising above their six; from Niggas, back to Gods/Divine Beings. The prince was respected by all, and I do mean 'all races', though some will not admit this fact. Malcolm was one of the biggest forces of the Civil Rights Movement in the 60's and 70's, even though he had already passed from this life to the next world.

He could not and would not be converted by the race of Necromongers, who came after him with a so-called reason to kill. They succeeded in killing him physically, but, in truth, he lives on. I see him and his dreams every day. We still have a long way to go before we achieve our ultimate goal.

One dream that still eludes us is the togetherness of black people. Malcolm X wanted us to be aggressive to our enemy and peaceful to each other. Here in 2013 we still have it ass-backwards. You may not agree with everything he said or did, but the truth is the results were positive. To this day, what he did for blacks is positive. You can't deny this, though many will still try.

Malcolm X deserves a day for his contributions just as Martin Luther King, Jr. has his day for his dream. Our prince heard our outcry just as Martin did. He helped organize blacks, bringing them together, rebirthing us through knowledge that had been lost centuries ago. So give him his day. "On May 19th, 1925, a prince was born in Omaha, Nebraska." His father was a black Freemason, just as my mother's father.

Elijah (Robert Pool) Muhammad was the founder of the lost, found nation of Islam and second father to our prince, Malcolm X. The honorable Elijah Muhammad was a black nationalist under the teachings of Marcus Garvy and later became a student of 'the Greatest Thief in the Night', the honorable Fard Muhammad. Fard came in sheep's clothing and stole one slave who was half-awake, opening his third eye, giving him sight beyond sight. This one so-called Negro/Necrot stole another and another, and another. Elijah became a master thief with the help of Marcus Garvy and Fard Muhammad, who in turn showed Malcolm how to be a master thief. The nation of Islam became a new home for many so-called Negros.

Elijah Muhammad wasn't at the forefront of things, but nonetheless he was there as he needed to be. He helped solve enigmas that had eluded blacks for ages, enigmas as to who they were and where they had come from. Most of all he restored a heritage that had been lost for hundreds of years.

You don't have to agree with what he did, but those days called for in-your-face reality checking and it worked. He taught us how to subdue the Jinn within us. No one is perfect. I can testify to that, with my strong cravings of the flesh if that's how you wish to phrase it.

Elijah's dream was for a lost people to go into themselves and understand the truth of self-worth. He wanted us to know ourselves. He proved to us through Malcolm and the Holy Qur'an that we exist. Then the nation gave us back our lost pride.

So once again, as you can see, Martin Luther King, Jr. wasn't the only contributor to the Civil Rights Movement of the 60's and 70's. These Necromongers would have us believe that Malcolm X gave nothing but hate.

Let us go back in time to Mother Moses, born Harriet Tubman. She was born into slavery, but didn't stay one for long. Mother Moses had a Ph.D. in Theifology when it came to freeing her people. Mother Moses' dream was to see the Negro slave freed from bondage, to see them with an education, to see their human rights respected. She wanted to see black and white children play together without being in fear of someone finding out about it. What Mother Moses did was give us the courage to hunger for freedom of all kinds, as well as a free-dom, a mind un-banded by the trick knowledge of Shaitan and William Lynch. She didn't risk her life for us so that we can do all the dumb things we do today. We have not only disrespected mother. We have spit in her eye, slapped her in the face, burned down her home and blown up the railroads she built.

The striving for our civil and human rights was being fought far before the 60's and 70's. Mother Moses was not only freeing our people from physical bondage. She was also freeing our minds, though she may not have known it at the time. She was setting the tone for future generations to come, setting the strength of those that would fight for our rights. We still have a long way to go to see her dream come completely true, but give her a day. Mother Moses put her work in. We owe her the respect due her.

Mother Moses is the Sangreal of us all. We must understand this truth and know (not believe, but know) that its due to Mother Moses and those like her for our ability to claim a mountain that seemed to high and dangerous at one point in time. Behind every black man there's a strong Mother Moses.

The Civil Rights Movement wasn't won by Martin Luther King, Jr. alone and he didn't start it, so people must give credit where credit is due. A movement is a resistance, which is a revolution, which is a movement. It can't be won by one person alone.

Mother Moses Lives On

Calmly the wind blows
      Across my soul
As she speaks the words
      That I'm sure to hang onto
She speaks words of wisdom
      And words of peace

Live on Mother Moses
      Live on

She laid the tracks to help me
      Escape the enslavement
Of my mental entrapment
      The chains that kept me bound
To my so-called master
      She has freed me

Just as the North Star
      Guides a lost child home
So too are women for men
      Of lost souls in a wicked world

Live on Mother Moses
      Live on

She is the key to my heaven
      I am the key to hers;
Giving up as we run for the finish line
      Isn't part of her plan

So she pushes me on
       I remain strong, because I know
Moses has my back

Live on Mother Moses
       Live on

They said Mother Moses is dead
       But, "Oh!" She says not
She lives on within the hearts and souls
       Of every black woman
And every little black girl

Live on Mother Moses
       Live on
Mother Moses
       Lives on.

Angela Davis, Afro-black Jacket, pumped her fist in the air and loudly declared, "I'm black and I'm proud!" This was, or should I say is, a sista who was up for a people's resistance by any means deemed necessary. As the revolution forged onward, sista Davis was there to be heard, letting us know it's time to wake up and stand strong, because it's going to be a bumpy ride.

She, along with Asanta Shakur, gave black women the positive image needed for the struggle. These daughters of Mother Moses helped lay the tracks so many of us walk on today. Sista Davis had a dream of seeing young black girls and boys growing up with a good education and better living conditions. Her contribution gave many youths the voice to say, "Yes I can!" She helped make it possible for blacks to become doctors, lawyers, judges, nurses, actors and actresses. There were few in her time, but many more followed, because she dared to resist the powers at hand, who were trying to prevent the re-genesis of the black strength and pride of our ancestors.

Ms. Davis is, and was, a part of the Panther 21, which was thrown in jail on charges of murder. The charges against her were later dropped. I personally thank this modern-day Mother Moses for taking the time to be a part of the resistance, for helping give us a much needed voice. We still have a lot of work to do, but sista Davis sleeps easier today.

The revolution doesn't start or stop with Martin Luther King, Jr. We should give credit where credit is always due. Yes, Martin was a good man, but he wasn't the only one with a great dream for our future. Mother Moses/Angela Davis had the same dream, so give her a day. She has earned that too. Yet these Necromongers would have us believe she gave nothing, that it's the non-violent marches that won it all.

Mother Black Panther, "Asanta Shakur", was also a part of the great resistance in the 60's and 70's. She gave an image to uphold for all black women of that time and black women in the future. Mother Panther gave lost black boys a mother to be proud of and little black girls a mother to model themselves after. Asanta had a dream as well. She stood strong to make sure it came true. She is from the royal blood of Mother Moses. She set the future track for me, and all to come, to follow. For all the work she has put in, we are showing great disrespect.

Yes, we've done some good, but we still have a long way to go, with little time left to achieve the goal. Whatever we are going to do, we need to do it now. We must ask Mother Panther to forgive the outright disrespect shown to her and her family of Panthers, many of whom died for our rights.

Asanta Shakur wanted young brothas and sistas to be more than a ghetto-born child. Mother Panther is one of the mothers of the Panthers who help make it possible for "Big O" President Obama to be president and "Mother MO" Michelle Obama to be the first lady.

Martin Luther King, Jr. wasn't the only one in the movement of the 60's and 70's. MLK died in '68, three years after Malcolm's passing. Both live on. We must give credit where credit is due. You can best know that Asanta "Mother Black Panther" Shakur has earned that respect, so give her a day. Yet these Necromongers would have us believe she was not fighting for us, that Mother Panther didn't really exist. They would have you believe her contribution to the resistance had no great impact on the issues in her day. We owe Mother Panther and her cubs much.

The sun didn't rise or set on brotha Martin's ass, so stop acting like it did and give credit to all who dared to resist. We know who pulled the triggers, but we also know who set the good brotha up for it to happen.

By the Hands of Blackmen

For far too long my people have been
        Dying for nothing with meaning
Young and old
        This craziness has gotten old
What were our ancestors fighting for?
        If this is how it's going to end
The revolution of the 60's and 70's
        Didn't stop there
We still have a war to win
        We need every soldier we can get
But they're dying off by the hands
        Of blackmen.
By the hands of blackmen
        We have killed more of our own
Then slavery ever did
        Trust me when I say that mentally
Willy Lynch must die
        Psychological slavery
And mental warfare
        Still plague the minds of many
So we must each one teach one
        By the hands of blackmen
We build up a nation
        And by the hands of blackmen
We will tear it down
        Without a thought of making it
Our own
        It's the mental warfare that got us
Thinking this way.

By the hands of blackmen
        We must raise our children
By the seven laws of Kwanzaa
        Teach them how to eat, to live
Give them a loving home and guide
        Them the right way
Because it is they who will lead us
        Into the future
They know more than what we
        Give them credit for.
By the hands of blackmen
        We must love our women
Not beat our women
        Help our women
Not leave our women
        Destroy the lie that all blackmen
Are dogs and don't know how to
        Love our beautiful black
Nubian Queens.

By the hands of blackmen
        There will be a better tomorrow.
By the hands of blackmen
        We shall live on and die no more.
By the hands of blackmen
        We will rise up and be the Gods
And Earths we were created to be.

By the hands of blackmen
        By the hands of blackmen
           By,
           The hands,
           Of BLACKMEN.

August 30, 1948 was the date of the birth of a good brotha by the name of Fred Hampton. He was born in Chicago and became a force for the Black Panthers Chapter, which was based in Chi Town. Yes, we know that white police shot and murdered him in his own home while he was in bed with poison running through his veins. A so-called brotha "black man" had put the poison in his drink or food. In truth this brotha, like our prince Malcolm "X" Shabazz was murdered by the hands of a black man. Brotha Hampton became a part of the movement, because he too had a dream so that his then unborn son would have a better tomorrow, with a good education, better living, a great job and dreams of his own.

Unlike many who converted for fame or fortune, he was unconvertible, so the Necromongers killed him. Hampton dreamed of a better future for every black man, woman and child.

Give this very good brotha his credit for the resistance/revolution of the 60's and 70's. When the choice to fight was handed to him, he ran with it, only thinking of a better tomorrow for us all. Now his widow and son stay in Oakland, California. As I stated before, Dr. King wasn't the only person within the resistance. There were many people that gave their lives as well. They all deserve credit for their contributions. Our today is okay, but our future tomorrow could be so much better. The struggle wages on.

Thank you brotha!

Now let me say that I don't take Dr. King's contribution lightly at all. He was a part of the movement in his own way: non-violence. I don't agree on how he did things, but as I said, "There is no one way to fight in a rebellion, battle, resistance, war, struggle or revolution." Everyone isn't cut out to be a soldier/warrior in the physical sense. One must find their own way to contribute to a resistance/revolution.

One must understand that Dr. King wasn't assassinated because he was no real threat. He was assassinated, because he was a very real threat to the goals that the Necromongers had been working towards. Dr. King had worn out his welcome and usefulness to the powers that be. Had he kept away from militant Christians who were willing to fight physically against our oppressors, he may still be with us. I don't see how one can win a savage war, battle, resistance or revolution by not fighting back, yet being violent toward their own.

The savage way we are toward each other is the most violent slap in the face to those that risked their lives and freedom for what little we have today. At the rate we're going, we'll annihilate ourselves out of existence. We cannot and must not keep going down the road to nowhere fast. We can't only be black one month out of the year or on Martin Luther King's birthday, Kwanzaa, or when convenient. Our heritage doesn't change. It is what it is 365 days out of the year. Therefore, our heritage needs to be celebrated 365 days a year.

There is nothing wrong with Black Nationalism as long as it's done without bigotry and prejudice. Now to me, racism is the same as nationalism. Being a bigot or prejudiced person is a twisted form of what racism really is. In the dictionary, look for Nationalism, racism, race, nation, ism and ist. First let's take a look at the meaning of Nationalism.

> **Nationalism**: 1. Devotion to the interests of culture of a particular nation 2. Aspirations for national independence.

Definition one of nationalism states, "Devotion to the interests of culture of a particular nation." Now as I have stated before, we are a nation, a family. It takes all of us working together to make our nation strong. Family means together, okay. Togetherness as one means that we are devoted to the betterment of our people, Malcolm Shabazz, Asanta Shakur, Elijah Muhammad, Angela Davis, Fred Hampton, BPP, BCP, Move Movement, BLA, etc. They all fought for the lost and much needed culture of a lost nation. We needed discipline, needed to be educated as well as re-educated, needed to be mentally enlightened and lifted up from the shackles of the psychological slavery we are in to this day. We need this even more so in these present times.

The beliefs we have are not the beliefs of our ancestors. They are the beliefs of a people who believe themselves superior to everyone else. The fighters all fought for the right to be treated as human beings. Many died for us to have this right.

Prince Malcolm showed that we as a people have a most genius intellect, which is untouchable if we are mentally trained in discipline and educated the right way. Like many others, our prince cultured himself with the blessing of the Most High. Once he was out of prison, the honorable Elijah Muhammad helped with what else was needed. All other members of the movement did the same thing. They led by example.

In definition two, you read, "The aspirations for national independence." The hopes and dreams of being an independent race of people in a land our ancestors built is another reason for the struggle of the 60's and 70's.

Which race of people was the revolution for? It was for a black people who are the descendants of slaves. They were fighting for a people with a dark pigmented skin tone, a dark nation if you will. They didn't just fight for their own rights, because we come from a race of people who are strong and created in the likeness of God. Who was this race of people they found so very impelled to fight for and why? Go to the word race and see the meaning.

> **Race**: 1. The descendants of the same ancestor; a family, tribe or people; breed; as, the human race. 2. State of being one of a particular race.

The slogan was, "Say it loud. I'm black and I'm proud." That was back in the 60's and 70's when there was real racial pride taught to us by those mentioned here in this book. They knew that we are all descendants of slaves from so-called Africa. We have the ancestors' particular blood, which we belong to as the so-called African Race, which is actually Kemet, Cush, Kibulaan, etc. Their fight was our fight and our fight is/was their fight. The enlightenment of a people is/was a must, but we have a problem. Today black people don't know they exist nor even believe they exist and that makes us the walking Necrot. You must first believe you exist, before you can really know you exist. To know would mean you have knowledge of, or the facts of, that which is true. Remember, "*Knowledge is exalted over belief.*"

When you know you exist, you then know that the rest of your family exists. Then you'll know what to fight for, and why you're fighting. All the people mentioned in this chapter were enlightened to their existence. Therefore they knew we exist and what to fight for. We all came from the same descendants. We all have the same family ties in some shape, form or fashion. They knew our nationality was the same, which makes us a nation. Who understands this fact better than the lost, found nation of Islam, the Five Percent Nation and the Black Moors of America?

Let's look at nation if you will.

> **Nation**: 1. A relatively large group of people organized under a single government. 2. A people; nationality. 3. A federation or tribe.

The definition of what a nation is applies to the nation of Islam, the Five Percent Nation and the Black Moors of America, as well as the following.

> BPP (Black Panther Party)
> BLA (Black Liberation Army)
> BCP (Black Communist Party)
> BSP (Black Socialist Party)
> The Move Movement
> OAU (Organization of African Unity)
> OAAU (Organization of African American Unity)

They all came under one governing body, organizing a lost people to lift up and enlighten them, people of the same nationality. These imps, Necromongers and incubi are a danger to us all. Our women had fallen victim to them and it is a recurring nightmare to the rest of us. There is no difference between the US government and the groups mentioned.

No nation has ever won its independence without a revolution, resistance, rebellion, battle or war. Just like the US, they all have or had their isms, which they stood and still stand by. Now what is an ism?

>**Islam**: 1. A distinctive doctrine, system, theory, principles and school of thought.

A very good example of a distinctive doctrine is Kwanzaa and its seven laws:

>IMANI-Faith
>UMOJA-Unity
>KUJICHAGULIA-Self determination
>UJIMA-Collective work and responsibility
>UJAMAA-Cooperative economics
>NIA-Purpose
>KUUMBA-Creativity

>*See book one of Uthman

The theory is that if we as a people would follow the principles of Kwanzaa or that of NOI, %5 Nation, BPP or OAAU, we as a people would grow stronger on every level of our existence. Now take book one of Uthman for example. This book is in many ways a school of thought by many who know it to be true. Christianity is also a school of thought. So is Buddhism, Hinduism, Zen, etc. These are all schools of thought and they each have their own system, principles and theories.

If you follow the isms of the governing body you so happen to be introduced to or just believe in some of what's being pushed, then you are of the ism. If you help push the isms of your people and you guys are of a particular race, that in itself reveals that you partake in racism, which makes you a racist all; because you love your people (race) and are willing to do what it takes to see your folks on top, doing good for themselves. It's racist, yet it doesn't make you prejudiced.

Whites teach generation after generation their own schools of thought, theories, principles and systems for the betterment of their people (race). That is, if I'm not mistaken, Nationalism for a particular nationality of people who themselves are a nation, which is a family. Now call my crazy, but that's racism.

Wouldn't that make them racist? I never once, as of yet, said that makes them bigots or prejudiced, even though many do believe they are superior to other races. That false superiority is twisted thinking. They would have us believe that racism is a bad thing, as well as Nationalism, yet they teach their young ones the very same things every day, yet tell you and me that it's wrong. They called people of the movement, who were willing to do anything to come out on top or speak out against their oppressors, extremist. If I'm not mistaken again, isn't that how the US gained its independence and was able to become the leading world power. Maybe it's just my imagination.

If it's right for them, how is it wrong for us to teach and be of the same ism? I have thirteen children by ten women and one of my children has a white mother. I also have a great aunt who's white. My grandparents on both sides of the family have Native American blood. I'm the last one to be called prejudiced. Not to mention I have a cousin that's black and Mexican. Shit, I'm a walking rainbow. Therefore, I have no right to be a bigot or prejudiced toward anyone, but I do love my black people. I have the true knowledge (isms) of my people, with which I stand by, but in no way am I prejudiced.

Malcolm, Angela, Asanta, Elijah and Fred all knew that what I'm saying is true. What do you think the resistance/revolution was about? It's the same as what Dr. King was fighting for, nothing different. As said before, Dr. King wasn't the only one trying to achieve a goal for a people he so loved.

There was more than one person involved in the laying of the path we now walk upon. Give them all credit for what they did, which was enabling many black people to get ahead in life. It wasn't just Martin Luther King's dream to one day have a black president. It was all their dreams, even more so for Prince Malcolm X. Malcolm had a white teacher who asked him what he wanted to be when he grew up. He replied, "The president of the United States of America." That dream didn't belong to just Dr. King.

We lay asleep among the ashes of our ancestors. It's about time to dance the dance of Necromancy in order to speak with the dead, the souls of those that have passed on. Before we reemerge out of the ashes like the great Phoenix, let our ancestors guide us in the way we must go, let them show us what it is we need to see, let them make us strong once again.

Notes:

Let Us Be the Phoenix

We must rise from the ashes
      Of our past
It's said that which
      Does not kill us
Only makes us stronger

Let us be the Phoenix

Through the ages
      We have been mis-educated
Forced into slumber
      Told we could never be

A once great people
      Made greater in the eyes of mankind
But the truth we do not see
      Because our minds are so ghetto
Let us build upon the truth
      And destroy all lies
Let us rise
      Let us rise

Let us be the Phoenix

Deaf, dumb and blind we are
      To the very truths around us
A truth we all must come to
      Is that Willy Lynch must die
We must awaken and rise

Let us be the Phoenix

Let us spread our wings
            Arise from the ashes of our
Tormented ancestors souls
            And be the restorers
Of our great kingdom

You are the Phoenix
            I am the Phoenix
We are the Phoenix
            Let us rise from their ashes

        Let us be the Phoenix.
        We cannot allow the past struggles of those before us to be all for a lie. There is no way we, as black people in 2013, should still be struggling harder than we were in the 50's, 60's, 70's and 80's. The 80's weren't that bad financially for us. We don't just owe it to ourselves to make a better tomorrow. We owe it to our ancestors of years past, to all of us, to all people.
        Psychological slavery is far worse than physical slavery ever was, because at least the enemy was easy to pinpoint when it was physical. Now it's hard for many of us to find the true enemy, due to there being so many road blocks. These road blocks can be moved, though. Someone must show us how to move them. Without the right knowledge, we can't go forward, nor will we be able to help the resistance in any way.
        There must be an end to these delusions of grandeur. None of us is any more important than the other, no matter how much money you have. If you really feel so, let me tell you a truth you need to know. "You are a legend in your own mind."
        These Necromongers are only as strong as you allow them to be. We have to break the chains of psychological slavery. The one way to do this is by knowing thyself. Every time one of us breaks the chains and awakens, the beast gets weaker and

weaker, until it loses its hold on us all. We must awaken, rise from the ashes of our ghetto mentality and take hold of our lives. God did say, "There will be no help for lost people until they first help themselves."

Before I end here, just remember that there was more than one person fighting for us in the revolution of the 60's and 70's. Martin Luther King, Jr. didn't do it all. He wasn't the only one with a dream.

Notes:

Giving Them a Better Future

What we do today, determines
How the future will treat
Our children, tomorrow.
-James A Evans, Sr.

"Children should be seen, not heard." That dumb-ass saying is the reason why so many youth are caught up in drugs and gangs. They're seen, but never heard. Therefore, in the name of rebellion to parents, teachers and all authority, they act out in a most negative way. It's the only way they know how to be seen, in the hopes someone would be willing to hear their voice. Look at it as a mutated temper tantrum. We've all had them in some shape or form. The future isn't ours. It belongs to them. What we do today, determines what the future will hold for them. Who are we to deny them a better tomorrow?

We men and women must understand that without coming to some kind of common ground and respect with our children, neither one of us will have a positive future. The line of communication between parent and child isn't as strong as it should be. The key to any relationship is the one thing that missing. That's communication. It is even more important between parent and child, child and parent.

It doesn't matter if you think you have God in your life. You can be Muslim, Buddhist, Christian, Hindu, etc. However, the way you communicate with your child, speaks volumes as to how God fearing you really are. Verbal communication is not the only way to talk with your children. Our actions speak louder than words. If you use gestures or body language to show how you feel, you may wish to watch what your body says. If done wrong, you could be saying, "I hate you. You can do nothing. You're dumb." You could say a host of other negative things. You could say this with your body, when what you want to say is, "I love you. You brighten my day. I'm proud of you."

If you expected positive things out of your child, then you end up with this: "Hell tells the captain." You may want to check over the knowledge you've put into your child. Most of the time, what you put into them (education, wisdom, truths, knowledge, etc.) is mostly what you'll get out of them.

There will be many mistakes made and that's where we as parents come in. However don't browbeat your children, because that doesn't work and never has for anyone, young or old. Children are the future for us all. We must watch what we do and say around them. We must find balance within ourselves, because, if not, our children will repeat our mistakes as well as make their own. By then it's a case of Déjà vu for us and for generations to come, until the cycle is broken.

Giving them a better tomorrow is much easier than one would think. Unless we want our children to end up six and ten, we better go from can't-get-right to I-got-right. Go to your child or children and place your hand over their heart(s). Feel the blessed rhythm of their existence. Feel the beat of your future, our future, the future of every black man and woman on this earth.

Negativity doesn't always breed negativity. In many cases the very negative things around a child can make them go in a most positive direction. Yet we mustn't hope for that to happen. It's on us as parents to make sure they take the positive path, the road to somewhere good in the future. It remains open.

We tend to have unknown bitterness that we take out on our children. We do this, because we don't understand the backlash that is going to happen or could happen. Some of us tell our future they are nothing, that they're dumb and stupid, or threaten to send them away. Some of us try to send them away. One parent turns the child against the other parent. The latter has a very negative effect on the child's outlook for the days ahead.

If we want our children to have a better tomorrow, we must watch what we say around them. We can't be walking contradictions to our young ones. You and I as parents must lead by example. We must really listen to our future as they speak. We must guide them the best we can.

Backwards thinking like children are to be seen and not heard is bullshit. Look where it has gotten you, gotten them, gotten us. "*Children are to be seen and heard.*" We have to talk *with* our children, not *at* them. We have to learn to be a friend to them, but always a parent first. We must do all that is necessary to make sure this race of Necromongers doesn't take hold of their souls, because getting them back doesn't always happen like we want it to. When you do drugs, smoke or use unmanaged words when speaking, don't be shocked when your child turns out just as ass-backwards as you were. We owe children more respect than we've given them. Ignorance breeds ignorance.

How do you view your child or children? Sit back and think about it. I'm more than sure that for every positive point of view, there're as many negative outlooks to match four times over. A big no-no is teaching children the twisted form of racism, because you're not only closing avenues and doors for them, you're leading them away from blessings and Heaven's gates.

Browbeating your children and bullshit like tough love does them no good, nor does it do us any good. Many times children have insights we don't have or need help seeing. Education starts with the parents at home, not when they enter school at five or six years old. Our futures should learn from us the ABC's and 123's, along with spelling by the time they get to grade K. We should all give them a head start.

You should show your child that sports aren't the only professions that can get them out of the ghettos, projects and slums they grew up in. Too much browbeating in time will make a young one stop listening over time. We can't always expect others to do our job, although it takes a tribe to raise a child. However it's the direct line of parenthood to the child or children that they benefit from the most, in many cases.

A father's knowledge, insight, wisdom, truth and understanding to his young ones go a long way and it means the world to them, more than we know. A mother's hug, kiss, quality time, pat on the back and every encouraging word from her, means a lot to children. I know it did to me and I know it did to you too.

However we can be the Necromongers without realizing it, because death can come in many different forms. The mental death caused by one's own hand is far worse than any physical death. If you're mentally dead, then your soul is dead. The good news is that it can be resurrected by knowledge, the right kind of knowledge, pure knowledge (as in 360 degrees). When one has awakened fully from a death of the mind and soul, that one has resurrected oneself from the grave that one put oneself in.

Let their dreams be our dreams for a better tomorrow. Let our dreams be their dreams for a future that will keep us all in the graceful hands of the Most High. "Just because they are children doesn't mean their dreams are meaningless. We should care."

Dreams of a Child

Betrayed at birth and before he was born
By the ones who said they would love him forever

The wrath of a child has become
More and more dear as time goes by
He dreams of love
He dreams of Peace
He dreams of growing up
          and becoming someone one day
The dreams of a child is what keeps

The world going 'round
The child always dreams of being held
Within the loving arms of his mother
And being happy to hear the wise words
Of his father

He dreams of the days of his playful youth
He dreams of the day when all his pains
Will come to an end

He dreams

He dreams

But what does it matter to you anyway
For these are just the dreams of a child.

In case my point was not made, let me show you how leading by example for our children is important. Something I've learned through trial and error is that we will continue to go through bullshit, generation after generation, if we don't stop this déjà vu.

We all go through our own personal déjà vu every day we see our children. You tell your children never to smoke, yet there you are, smoking. Therefore, later on in their lives, they themselves smoke; déjà vu. You tell your children to never use bad language, but years later, when you're not around, they're using words that would make you want to run and hide; déjà vu. A man tells his son he should never, ever, hit a woman, yet the man is doing so. In that case, the son most often grows up hitting women; déjà vu. A woman tells her daughter that she better not go whoring around, yet the mother has men coming in and out of the house from sun up to sun down. Now the daughter has a pimp, or she is her own pimp; déjà vu. The same goes for stealing, robbing, killing, gang banging, selling drugs, etc., case in point.

In 1970, my father Carl Evans James, Sr. went to prison in Chicago for robbery and got out in 1975. My brother Carl J Evans, Jr. started going to jail early in life, landing in prison. He's 7'3", could have played ball, but he had other plans. In 2008 or 2007, he paroled from San Quentin Prison in his late 40's. Now here I am in prison (written in 2011). I first got locked up at 19 years old in 1990. Now it's 2011 (I'm 40 years old). In 2005, my eldest son James, Jr. was on 3B yard at Corcoran with two strikes. He can rap. I'll never forget the mix he made for me while I was studying Islam. Everyone knew me as Brother Uthman. They had always said Jr. and me looked alike. One day a correctional officer called for inmate Evans. Three people answered. Then he said, "James Evans." All three of us answered again. The officer then said, "James Allen Evans." One brotha said, "Well, it's not me. I'm out." We all laughed, but me and the other inmate identified as James Allen Evans. I said to the other,

"Look man, I don't know who you are, but I'll talk to you in the morning. There's only one James Allen Evans and that's me."

The young brotha called back, "Say dude, you got me fucked up. I'm named after my daddy." All went silent. Then brotha Kadi says, "Brotha Uthman, remember I said the two of you look alike?" I answered, "Yes." Brotha Kadi says, "Well brotha... that's your son you're talkin' too."

This event was my case of déjà vu. Another time in Corcoran, my second eldest son James Berry arrived as an inmate. Again my nightmare déjà vu visited me. That was in 2006. So far my father, my brother Carl, myself, my eldest son and my second eldest son, landed in prison; déjà vu. Although we are our own individuals, it's still a nightmare déjà vu for my father, because the saga continues. Unless the cycle stops now, this will go on for generations to come. My father's déjà vu has become my own.

If we want to give our children a better future, we must start by leading as a positive example. Don't let our young ones repeat our many mistakes by teaching hate, ignorance, contradictory thought and all out lies. Before we attempt to clean them up, let us first clean our own act up. Then they will follow a good path, a good path we first set for ourselves.

Blinding ignorance misleads us all. "O, wretched mortals. Open your eyes," said Leonardo DaVinci some time ago. We keep going through the dramas of past years, because of our refusal to believe it won't happen to us or our mistaken belief that déjà vu doesn't exist. What do we owe ourselves? We owe ourselves truth, loyalty, honesty, love and respect. We owe not only ourselves this, but our children as well. It doesn't matter if they're ours or not, it takes a tribe to raise one child. Let not our déjà vu be the déjà vu of our young ones.

Notes:

_____

_____

_____

_____

_____

_____

_____

_____

_____

_____

_____

_____

_____

_____

_____

_____

_____

_____

_____

_____

Knowledge

How do we stop from falling into the same old patterns that have gotten us nowhere fast? We do it by knowing thyself. You cannot know the Supreme Being if you don't know who you are. You cannot understand the future if you can't understand your past. Without understanding, our present becomes meaningless. What good is a gift, if we don't know why it was given to us?

Firstly, knowledge is exalted over belief. What I'm offering is the truth of your being. Knowledge is the act of knowing a fact. Knowing what is to be fact is the question. You can know many things, but is your knowledge the right knowledge? Knowledge is one thing that should not be taken lightly, which most of us tend to do. It can either help or harm you.

I don't care if the leader of your church tells you something comforting. Don't take his or her word for it, because that, my people, is harmful knowledge. That knowledge is an assumed fact. All it does is sound good. Here's the difference between belief and pure, righteous knowledge.

First you have the word know.

> **Know**: 1. To be certain of facts of truth of something, to understand clearly. 2. To be acquainted or familiar with truth.

The second word in knowledge is ledge.

> **Ledge**: 1. A flat space like a shelf in the side of a cliff or rock wall. 2. A narrow shelf that juts out from a wall.

It's said that the path to truth is narrow, where the path of lies is wide. The act of assuming is a belief and a belief is a wide lie. No one should ever have a belief, because it's an assumed fact. When you ask your church elder a question, nine times out of ten his or her answer is, "I don't know. You just need to believe." You want me to just ass/u/me you're right without question. It's not God I'm questioning. It's you and your teachings.

Blind faith is the same as having a belief, believing without question. That's ignorance. When you're told to just believe, here's what you're doing.

> **Belief**: 1. A thing or idea that is considered to be true, a belief in God. 2. A strong opinion or expectation.

Within that breakdown you have two other words: opinion and expectation.

> **Opinion**: 1. A belief based on what one thinks or feels, rather than actual facts.

> **Expectation**: 1. The act of assuming. 2. To assume. 3. To take for granted.

Well, I took for granted that the truth would be told when I stepped into the court room. I thought that I would go home. Since I ass/u/me(d), I got more time than I knew what to do with. Justice is truly blind. My belief in it got me put back in prison. Blind faith and belief is all out of ignorance. A belief is a contradiction waiting to happen.

To know or have knowledge of something is to be conscious of the truth or to have awareness of S.E.L.F. Your soul is a Supreme Eternal Life Form. This is a fact, not an ass/u/me(d) fact. You're now at the narrow shelf (ledge) of knowing.

56

You may be one who says, "I know God, but I'm still looking for the truth." You may further go out to teach the so-called Word of the Supreme Being. If you are that one, I use young brotha Fabian Hemphill's (Mr. Koo-Koo K-42982) words from a song of his called "What if I played God": "If it's the truth that you seek, then the words that you speak are all a mask of what you really don't know."

Who are you? Where do you come from? Once you find the answers to these questions, you are then the captain of your own destiny, the owner of your own soul. Another way to put it is, Islam is who we all are. ISLAM (I Self Lord And Master). We are the image and likeness of He Who hath created us.

Genesis 1:26-27

26. And God said let Us make man in Our Own image, after Our likeness.

27. So God created man in His Own image, in the image of God created He him.

Genesis 2:7. And the Lord God formed man of the dust of the ground, and breathed into his nostrils the breath of life and man became a living soul.

In the dictionary image and likeness are broken down so pay attention.

> **Image**: 1. A reproduction of a person or thing, especially a statue. 2. Something or someone that looks very much like another.

> **Likeness**: 1. Similarity. 2. In character within

We are a small copy of the Supreme Being, just as our children are small copies of ourselves. They are the reproduction of the Supreme Being with like character. We are more powerful than our children. We know what they don't know. Our physical strength may run short, but mentally and knowledge-wise we are stronger. They always want to know what we know, just as we always wish to know what our Creator knows. Look in a mirror and you'll see the image of God, the Most High, who loving, forgiving, creative, punishing, etc. performs His divine works. We as God-like beings have the same characteristics. We were made in the image and likeness of our Maker.

One must see the facts for what they are: facts. "In the beginning there was the word and the word was with God and the word is God." This word is and was "be," for God need only speak and it exists. Whatever he wills he only needs to say, "Be," and it is.

We are the word "be", because we are human (be)ings. Jesus isn't the only existing Being. The dictionary breaks be and being down as such.

Being: 1. A living creature. 2. Existence. 3. A person

Be: 1. To exist, live. 2. To occupy a certain position. 3. To take place, occur.

We were all with God before our flesh was created. Our existence occurred at the beginning of time. Our physical being took place here on earth at the time of its beginning. Our S.E.L.F. was created long before the physical self, came into existence to occupy the earth. Our soul was placed in the seed of our father and that seed became a person. We have an individual soul that was given to us on the day of our creation. We have what is called free will.

Remember the sayings of Christians and Nation Muslims: "I am the captain of my destiny. I am the owner of my soul." (Christians). "I Self Lord And Master." (Nation Muslims). Each knows of their given free will from Jehovah, Allah, Most High, Supreme Being, Yahweh, etc.

Y.O.U. are Your Own Universe. Within each individual's universe there is a strong magnetic pull. For some it's light as air and seems not to exist, but it's there all the same. This you can count on. If your soul's equilibrium is off balance, then there's no telling what your magnetic charge will pull into your universe. We can be the cause of our own negative pull. When you go left and your S.E.L.F. told you to go right, you end up in a ditch. It's on you for not listening to the S.E.L.F. However we can change a negative into a positive by the things we do, the people we hang around and the knowledge contained within our minds. The gravitational pull of our universes works one way. Respect the S.E.L.F. and the S.E.L.F. will respect Y.O.U.

Notes:

Atom I Am

I am the nucleus
From which all things exist
The self-existing
Who has will of creation

"Atom I am"
The beginning and the end
The Alpha and the Omega
I am the self-existing life form

"Atom I am"
You cannot know me unless
You know thyself
Without my beginning
There is no ending
There can be no beginning

"Atom I am"
My fifth element
Is who helps me in
My constant evolution
Through life
I am the electro-magnetic
Pulse of your existence

"Atom I am"
You have been created
In the image and likeness
Of an eternal soul
You are ATOM, male and female

"ATOM I AM"
"KNOWLEDGE IS EXALTED OVER BELIEF"

Death Before Dawn

Today is February 12, 2012. I can say that our down point is on its way out the door. We have been in a mental and spiritual death for hundreds of years. We fought who we were, where we came from, where we were headed. Our third eye has been stripped from us. I have many times asked for guidance from above. What I didn't know was that the path I had been seeking had already been laid before my feet. We are all looking for something to illuminate our way, but the knowledge is right in front of us. The only way we can come out of our deaths is to gain a true consciousness for who we are. Then many things will be given unto us.

Knowledge and wisdom are given to all who are true in heart. Knowledge isn't for everyone. Look at the events today and see what people have done with knowledge.

The death of a nation began somewhere around 1568 with slavery, but our deaths started when we forgot the Most High. The many things we've gone through in life are due to the fact that we as a people have our backs turned, when we should be facing forward at all times.

The walking dead trance we seem to be in is on its way to turning around. We will find true, profound enlightenment. No matter how many times we may trip, stumble or fall, we must not lose focus, as we tend to do at times. When we do lose focus, that's when it is most important to hold our brothers and sisters close. When it's all said and done, if we stood strong, held still and moved as a nation, that promise land will be given to us.

It was very important for us to have this death, that we may reach our down point. It's you live and you learn. It's not you learn and you live. All I've written in these few pages was to offer you a step away from your mental and spiritual death. Your third eye is awakening.

What I have written was learned from the Holy Qur'an, the Holy Bible, Webster's Dictionary, History and a whole lot of common sense. No one has to agree with what I wrote, but I would ask that you study more and grab your bible, Qur'an or dictionary. Go back in the history books and see that none of what I said was untrue.

I have simplified these ideas to ensure an easy understanding. A three-year-old child could possibly understand what I have written. Form your own sound opinions. I'm sure you would have to agree. Many before me have come and said what I wrote in many different ways. Once one comes into knowing, he also comes into being. It then becomes his job to illuminate the way for the rest of mankind, for many are still dead and asleep.

I wrote these truths for all people, but mostly for my lost brothas and sistas, who are in drastic need of an awakening. You must seek knowledge from the cradle to the grave, no matter the place you must go to get it, no matter the book that hides it.

One book I highly suggest is "Secret Power of Words", written by Roy Masters. He's a Christian. I'm a Muslim, not the best, but I'm trying. As I have said, "No prejudice here."

Never be turned back around, because of someone telling you, "Oh! Now you want to gain knowledge when you did this or that." They may use your past to dissuade you.

It doesn't matter how or when you awaken. What matters is that now you are in the know. Your being is now breathing. Our dawn is surely at hand. It's a must that we wake up before we are left behind with the damned. Our dawn is a story told back in history, but our real dawn will be among the greatest of legends.

Never forget the past, but don't let it make you bitter and unfocused. Lost knowledge gained can and will cause anger to well up from within your soul. You will burn with a fury. Instead of using that anger unwisely, grow from what was done and what we failed to do. Do not dwell on it. Build my people. (Build) '3737 & 6'... Find your S.E.L.F. Learn and grow.

Notes:

Books to Buy

1. Holy Qur'an
2. Holy Bible
3. Secret Power of Words by Roy Masters
4. Know Thyself by Elijah Muhammad
5. Any book written by Malcolm X
6. 100 Amazing Facts About the Negro by J A Rogers
7. Community of Self by Na'im Akbar
8. From Niggas to Gods by unknown author
9. Books on Zen
10. Pawns in the Game by unknown author
11. Watch the movies "The Chronicles of Riddick" and "Red Planet"
12. Also watch "Dune"

Reading these would be a great start for those who are still in their deaths

Let your eternal cosmic order be seen in all its glory.

Notes:

Author's Bio

I was born 1971 in Omaha, Nebraska, May 24th to Betty C Evans and Carl J Evans, Sr. I met my father for the first time in 1975. Later in 1979 we all moved to California. My parents separated in 1980. My mother, my sister Felicia and I moved to Long Beach where we've been ever since. I'm an ex-gang member, ex-drug dealer, ex-drug user, ex-low-level-pimp, etc.

In 1990 at the age of 19 I went to prison for burglary with a sentence of 6 years. After the term I was released and married Veronica Totress of Carson, California. I have children by Shanda (Webb) Gwenn, Pamela Thomas and Correctional Counselor C Berry. 20 years of my life have been spent in prison. While incarcerated I studied and re-educated myself with the help of God. I was released from prison on May 24th 2011.

I earned a BA Degree in Human Behavior / Psychology, which was taken back, because I didn't get my GED within the two years I was given by Coastline Community College.

I now reside in the west side of Long Beach, CA in a sober living. I'm four months clean off drugs. I attend Deacon's class, bible study and church every Sunday. I occasionally teach Sunday school. I'm seeking to become an ordained minister. The church I attend is Way of Faith Christian Church. The current year is 2013.

CPSIA information can be obtained
at www.ICGtesting.com
Printed in the USA
BVHW090443110822
644264BV00007B/943

9 781622 873753